Your Government:
How It Works

The Central Intelligence Agency

Tara Baukus Mello

Arthur M. Schlesinger, jr.
Senior Consulting Editor

Chelsea House Publishers
Philadelphia

CHELSEA HOUSE PUBLISHERS
Editor in Chief Stephen Reginald
Production Manager Pamela Loos
Art Director Sara Davis
Director of Photography Judy L. Hasday
Managing Editor James D. Gallagher
Senior Production Editor LeeAnne Gelletly

Staff for THE CENTRAL INTELLIGENCE AGENCY
Project Editor/Publishing Coordinator Jim McAvoy
Associate Art Director Takeshi Takahashi
Series Designer Takeshi Takahashi, Keith Trego

The Chelsea House World Wide Web address is
http://www.chelseahouse.com

First Printing
1 3 5 7 9 8 6 4 2

Library of Congress Cataloging-in-Publication Data

Mello, Tara Baukus.
    The Central Intelligence Agency / by Tara Baukus Mello.
        p. cm. — (Your government—how it works)
    Includes bibliographical references and index.
    Summary: A behind-the-scenes look at the government agency
that analyzes information from all over the world to make sure
that the United States remains safe from attack by other countries
or terrorist groups.
    ISBN 0-7910-5531-0 (hc.)
    1. United States. Central Intelligence Agency—Juvenile litera-
ture. 2. Intelligence service—United States—Juvenile literature.
[1. United States. Central Intelligence Agency. 2. Intelligence
service. 3. Spies.] I. Title. II. Series.

JK468.I6.M455 2000
327.1273—dc21   99-048914

Contents

YOUR GOVERNMENT ★ **HOW IT WORKS**

Introduction

Government: Crises of Confidence

Arthur M. Schlesinger, jr.

FROM THE START, Americans have regarded their government with a mixture of reliance and mistrust. The men who founded the republic understood the importance of government. "If men were angels," observed the 51st Federalist Paper, "no government would be necessary." But men are not angels. Because human beings are subject to wicked as well as to noble impulses, government was deemed essential to assure freedom and order.

The American revolutionaries, however, also knew that government could become a source of injury and oppression. The men who gathered in Philadelphia in 1787 to write the Constitution therefore had two purposes in mind: They wanted to establish a strong central authority and to limit that central authority's capacity to abuse its power.

To prevent the abuse of power, the Founding Fathers wrote two basic principles into the Constitution. The principle of federalism divided power between the state governments and the central authority. The principle of the separation of powers subdivided the central authority itself into three branches—the executive, the legislative, and the judiciary—so that "each may be a check on the other."

YOUR GOVERNMENT: HOW IT WORKS examines some of the major parts of that central authority, the federal government. It explains how various officials, agencies, and departments operate and explores the political organizations that have grown up to serve the needs of government.

Introduction

The federal government as presented in the Constitution was more an idealistic construct than a practical administrative structure. It was barely functional when it came into being.

This was especially true of the executive branch. The Constitution did not describe the executive branch in any detail. After vesting executive power in the president, it assumed the existence of "executive departments" without specifying what these departments should be. Congress began defining their functions in 1789 by creating the Departments of State, Treasury, and War.

President Washington, assisted by Secretary of the Treasury Alexander Hamilton, equipped the infant republic with a working administrative structure. Congress also continued that process by creating more executive departments as they were needed.

Throughout the 19th century, the number of federal government workers increased at a consistently faster rate than did the population. Increasing concerns about the politicization of public service led to efforts—bitterly opposed by politicians—to reform it in the latter part of the century.

The 20th century saw considerable expansion of the federal establishment. More importantly, it saw growing impatience with bureaucracy in society as a whole.

The Great Depression during the 1930s confronted the nation with its greatest crisis since the Civil War. Under Franklin Roosevelt, the New Deal reshaped the federal government, assigning it a variety of new responsibilities and greatly expanding its regulatory functions. By 1940, the number of federal workers passed the 1 million mark.

Critics complained of big government and bureaucracy. Business owners resented federal regulation. Conservatives worried about the impact of paternalistic government on self-reliance, on community responsibility, and on economic and personal freedom.

When the United States entered World War II in 1941, government agencies focused their energies on supporting the war effort. By the end of World War II, federal civilian employment had risen to 3.8 million. With peace, the federal establishment declined to around 2 million in 1950. Then growth resumed, reaching 2.8 million by the 1980s.

A large part of this growth was the result of the national government assuming new functions such as: affirmative action in civil rights, environmental protection, and safety and health in the workplace.

Some critics became convinced that the national government was a steadily growing behemoth swallowing up the liberties of the people. The 1980s brought new intensity to the debate about government growth. Foes of Washington bureaucrats preferred local government, feeling it more responsive to popular needs.

But local government is characteristically the government of the locally powerful. Historically, the locally powerless have often won their human and constitutional rights by appealing to the national government. The national government has defended racial justice against local bigotry, upheld the Bill of Rights against local vigilantism, and protected natural resources from local greed. It has civilized industry and secured the rights of labor organizations. Had the states' rights creed prevailed, perhaps slavery would still exist in the United States.

Americans are still of two minds. When pollsters ask large, spacious questions—Do you think government has become too involved in your lives? Do you think government should stop regulating business?—a sizable majority opposes big government. But when asked specific questions about the practical work of government—Do you favor Social Security? Unemployment compensation? Medicare? Health and safety standards in factories? Environmental protection?—a sizable majority approves of intervention.

We do not like bureaucracy, but we cannot live without it. We need its genius for organizing the intricate details of our daily lives. Without bureaucracy, modern society would collapse. It would be impossible to run any of the large public and private organizations we depend on without bureaucracy's division of labor and hierarchy of authority. The challenge is to keep these necessary structures of our civilization flexible, efficient, and capable of innovation.

More than 200 years after the drafting of the Constitution, Americans still rely on government but also mistrust it. These attitudes continue to serve us well. What we mistrust, we are more likely to monitor. And government needs our constant attention if it is to avoid inefficiency, incompetence, and arbitrariness. Without our informed participation, it cannot serve us individually or help us as a people to attain the lofty goals of the Founding Fathers.

Columbine High School students comfort each other in the aftermath of the shootings. Unlike the students who had heard the shooters talk about their plans but said nothing, CIA employees are trained to know when secrets should be told.

CHAPTER 1

Keeping and Telling Secrets

THINK BACK TO A time when you knew a secret. Did anyone else know the secret too? Did you talk to that person about it? Did you tell the secret to anyone else?

With this secret you had special knowledge—information that very few people, perhaps no one else, knew. Maybe it was what you bought your mom for her birthday. Maybe it was that your older brother cheated on a big test. Or maybe it was something even more important.

What you decided to do with that special knowledge changed the course of history just a little bit. For example, if you told on your big brother for cheating on a test, he probably got in trouble. Your parents might have punished him, but it might have been even worse; maybe he was suspended from school. Either way, if you told his secret, his life would be different from what it would have been if no one knew he had cheated on the test.

A small secret like this may not seem very important, but it could be part of a bigger secret that could really hurt people and really change the course of history. On April 20, 1999, two students went on a shooting spree at Columbine High School in Littleton, Colorado. Many of the students and adults literally ran for their lives as bullets and bombs filled the school. In the end, 12 students and one teacher died, but every single person who was at that school had his or her life changed forever. All because of a secret plan between two students to go shooting that day.

Just as with many secrets, some students at Columbine High School had heard the two students talk about guns and bombs and had even heard them threaten to kill other students, but they did not believe the students would ever actually do it. Some of these students had special, or "secret," information—only they did not realize it until it was too late.

The Central Intelligence Agency, also called the CIA, is trained not only to learn secrets, but to know when they should be "told" or taken seriously. They have the training that the students at Columbine High School did not have, and that is what helps keep our country safe from harm by other countries.

The CIA is a government agency that analyzes information from all over the world to make sure that the United States remains safe from attack by other countries or terrorist groups. As individuals we learn lots of different secrets over our lifetimes, and it is up to us not only to decide whether to share the secret or to keep it to ourselves but also to decide if it is important information that should be shared.

At the CIA thousands of employees gather information from various sources and must decide what is true and important and then decide what they should do with the information. Working at the CIA is like being part of a giant family that spends everyday building a puzzle at the dining room table, only to learn that parts from other puzzles are mixed in too. Each day some family members bring different pieces of the puzzle to the table and try to make them fit somewhere. Everyday too, different family members take a few pieces out of the puzzle, deciding that they do not belong.

It is easy to see why it would be so hard to put a puzzle like this together, but it is even more complicated than that. This puzzle does not have just 500 or 1,000 pieces; it has over a trillion pieces. Each piece represents a tiny bit of information that the CIA has gathered from somewhere in the world. Some of the family members gather the puzzle pieces, other members provide tools to help gather or understand the pieces, and still others analyze them to decide if they are important.

Working at the CIA is like putting together a jigsaw puzzle of over a trillion pieces from thousands of different puzzles.

The CIA family also works with other government agencies to do their jobs better. This group of agencies is called the intelligence community, and the CIA is just one part of that community. There are 13 other government agencies, and each one has a different job in the information or intelligence process. As part of the intelligence community, the CIA provides accurate and timely information about things that might be a threat to the security of the United States. Sometimes they also perform **counterintelligence** activities, which are done to protect the secrets that the United States does not want foreign governments to learn. The CIA gathers information about only foreign people or countries, not about United States citizens.

All the work that the CIA does begins with a question from the president, the National Security Council, or a member of the cabinet. The questions asked might pertain to current events or information on the scientific or technical activities in a foreign country. Sometimes the CIA might be asked to provide the president or one of his key advisers with a lengthy report that studies a certain issue. At other times the CIA may need to draw conclusions from the information it has gathered and provide political leaders with a prediction on what they think might happen in the near or distant future. This type of intelligence is called estimative, or warning, intelligence.

The most famous group of people who work for the CIA are the operations officers. Most often called spies, they are the group that has been made famous through the movies and television. The life of a spy is very different from what you may see depicted in these media. Operations officers often work long hours, doing two jobs—their "cover" job and their "real" job of gathering, assessing, and analyzing information. Like the spies seen in the movies, they may wear a disguise, speak several languages, and use interesting gadgets, but their lives are not

Sean Connery as the first James Bond (Agent 007) helped create the popular image of spying as glamorous and highly adventurous.

nearly as glamorous. They may spend hours waiting or talking to people who don't end up giving them the information they need.

Operations officers rely on many people to help them do their jobs, including agents who bring them information. Most often agents are not CIA employees or even American citizens but people who have access to certain information and, for a variety of reasons, want to tell these secrets to the U.S. government. In addition to agents, the operations officers rely on many other people who work in other departments of the CIA to collect and analyze the

IN HONOR OF THOSE MEMBERS
OF THE CENTRAL INTELLIGENCE AGENCY
WHO GAVE THEIR LIVES IN THE SERVICE OF THEIR COUNTRY

The CIA memorial wall. The stars carved on its marble surface represent those killed in the line of duty. The book displayed beneath the stars lists the 25 names among them which can be revealed.

intelligence data. All these people working together assemble the pieces of that giant intelligence puzzle.

Most of the people who work at the CIA are not allowed to say they work there. Often even their children or other family members do not know that they work for the agency. Because much of what the CIA does is related to gathering secret information, it may not be in the news, or, if it is, another government agency may be credited with the information. Sometimes the people who make some of the most important contributions to the agency are never acknowledged by name to the outside world or even to other employees within the CIA.

In the lobby of the CIA headquarters in McLean, Virginia, is a marble wall. Chiseled in that wall are 77 stars, one for each person who has lost his or her life while serving the CIA. Below the stars is a book encased in glass. In this book of honor is a list of the people whose names can be revealed. All 77 people are heroes, but we know the names of just 25 of them. When the others died, they were working undercover and, as a result, the CIA will never reveal their identities.

As you read this book, you will get to meet some people, both famous and not so famous, who have had important roles in American intelligence. You will see some of the incredible gadgets that officers use in the field. You will learn what it is like to be part of the most elite group of CIA employees, the operations officers. You will even learn what it takes to get a job at the CIA and be able to decide for yourself if you would make the cut. Welcome to the Central Intelligence Agency, where it is their business to know the world's business.

R. Veenfliet.

George Washington commanding the Continental army in 1775. Washington's skillful information-gathering about British troop movements led him to be considered the father of American military intelligence.

CHAPTER **2**

I Spy, You Spy

ALTHOUGH THE CENTRAL INTELLIGENCE AGENCY is a relatively new organization, intelligence has been used and gathered throughout the world for thousands of years. George Washington, the first president of the United States, is considered to be the father of American military intelligence. In September 1776, at the beginning of the American Revolution, he formed Knowlton's Rangers, a group whose purpose was to gather information about the British soldiers' movements so the American troops would be able to prepare for the next battle.

Washington thought having advance information was so important that at first he recruited and trained his agents himself. It wasn't long, however, before Washington needed so much information that he hired a **case officer,** a person whose job was to find and train agents who would gather the information that Washington needed. In addition to gathering information, Washington sometimes put out incorrect information about his army in an effort to mislead the British troops. This is an example of counterintelligence, and Washington was an expert at it.

During the winter of 1777 at Morristown, New Jersey, Washington had some of his men tell two British officers that the American troops were much larger than they really were. Later he reinforced this information by using a **double agent,** a person who was working for both the American and British sides, to confirm the rumor. As a result the British leader, General Howe, believed it and decided not to attack.

By the fall of 1777, Washington had developed a good network of people who provided him with information, but it could have been even better. In fact, Washington lost the Battle of Brandywine Creek because his information about the terrain was completely incorrect. It was a small bit of information, but he nearly lost all of his troops as a result.

Washington's talents for counterintelligence are a big part of the reason that the Americans won the fight against the British in the war. In the final battle at Yorktown, Washington had created an elaborate plan to trick the British troops into thinking he was preparing to attack the British troops in New York City. In fact, the French Navy had joined the Americans and were getting ready to battle at Yorktown.

By the time of the Civil War, many people thought the Union and the Confederacy each had its own agencies that handled intelligence at the national level, but this was not true. On both sides intelligence gathering was the decision of the field commander, who could use as little or as many methods as he chose. Because there was no standard procedure for collecting intelligence, the responsibility of gathering military information could fall on many different people.

We do not know a lot about the gathering of intelligence during the Civil War, but historians think that there

were about 4,200 people on both the Union and Confederate sides that were involved in espionage. Many of these people were **scouts,** another word for spy. Because many scouts were civilians, they could choose between wearing civilian clothing or an enemy uniform when they went on a mission behind enemy lines.

General Washington's expert use of counterintelligence helped American troops win the final battle of the Revolution at Yorktown.

Both sides often gathered information through agents, although they used other methods as well. The Civil War was the first time that Americans used systematic military intelligence-gathering methods. These methods were a way for one side to monitor the movements of the other side. This was done, for example, by balloons (called aerial reconnaissance) or by intercepting the signals the troops were using to communicate. Other times prisoners were interrogated to gain information. Still another way both sides gathered intelligence was from **overt** sources, such as from refugees or from printed materials like newspapers.

Union Major General James B. McPherson and his staff pose in the field in this Civil War photograph. Generals from both sides needed the services of civilian spies when in enemy territory.

Intelligence became important for other countries as well as for the United States. Before World War I began, Germany had already created one of the most extensive intelligence units in the world, although they had done very little intelligence gathering in America. Once the war began, the Germans used a variety of covert actions against the United States. One of the methods the Germans used was buying up supplies and equipment in order to sabotage the Allies' operations.

During this time the British intelligence officers worked in America to try to counter the Germans' efforts and also to try to persuade the United States to join the Allied side of the war. One way that the British did this was by getting several German-made machines that deciphered messages and then intercepting and reading the messages that the Germans were sending.

At the beginning of the war, in 1914, the United States had few methods in place for gathering intelligence overseas. In addition, it did not have any national counterintelligence group to handle attacks on American intelligence. Soon, however, the army and navy created intelligence units in their headquarters in France and England. One group, called G-2, gathered military intelligence, such as maps and studies of the terrain. G-2 also performed radio intelligence activities, such as intercepting messages sent via radio, telephone, and carrier pigeon. Shortly after America entered World War I, President Wilson created a special intelligence group called "the Inquiry." The job of this group, which was mostly made up of college professors, was to study the problems that were inevitable once the war was over.

Since the 1890s, America had seen Japan as a threat and the Office of Naval Intelligence had even made a plan

Intelligence-gathering units, including President Woodrow Wilson's "the Inquiry," were created to meet the need for overseas intelligence and counterintelligence as the United States entered World War I.

for war with Japan, which was updated regularly until the 1930s. As a result, both the army's and navy's intelligence units monitored Japan's activities. As World War II approached, the navy intercepted and deciphered many of the Japanese communications. The army concentrated their efforts in this area as well, and, in 1940, they broke the code for the Japanese **cipher** machine they secretly called "purple."

Also in that year President Roosevelt sent William Donovan, a lawyer and World War I veteran, on a few secret fact-finding missions to England and the Mediterranean to gather information about the countries involved in the war. When Donovan returned he recommended to President Roosevelt that there be a central agency that controlled all covert activities and foreign intelligence reporting directly to the president. On July 11, 1941, the president created this unit with the new coordinator of information, William Donovan, as its head.

The Office of the Coordinator of Information, also called the COI, covered four main areas. These were (1) secret intelligence, which clandestinely collected intelligence; (2) research and analysis, which analyzed the intelligence gathered; (3) the foreign information service, which produced propaganda (pieces of information that made inaccurate claims); (4) and special operations, which performed covert operations.

Between the army, the navy, and the COI, the United States had gathered a lot of information about the activities of the Japanese. It was, however, still caught off guard when the Japanese attacked Pearl Harbor on December 7, 1941. If the United States had gathered its intelligence differently, this incident might have been prevented. Although agents had intercepted and decoded many of the Japanese messages, they had not linked the pieces together to see the warning signs of the attack. The United States had, in

fact, enough information to be warned of the Pearl Harbor attack. Unfortunately, however, there was a rivalry between the organizations gathering information and no one group had all of the information that had been gathered, so no one could accurately analyze the information.

After the Pearl Harbor incident, the COI and the military's intelligence units were forced to work together more closely. In June 1942 President Roosevelt renamed the COI the Office of Strategic Services, also known as the OSS, and had it report to the Joint Chiefs of Staff. This agency was designed to operate during the war as a central unit for intelligence, propaganda, and other **clandestine,** or secret, activities. The OSS operated throughout the war on a variety of missions that helped the Allied forces win the war, but the unit also helped shape the future of American intelligence.

If intelligence-gathering about Japanese activities had been properly coordinated, the United States would not have been caught off guard by the Japanese attack on Pearl Harbor.

As a result of the OSS's activities, intelligence work was viewed as a distinguished profession, in the way that being a diplomat or military officer would be considered prestigious. Similarly, clandestine activities became an accepted method of international relations. With the OSS began the concept of a single, high-level agency that organized all intelligence at a national level. It eventually evolved into the CIA we know today.

In September 1945 President Truman dissolved the OSS. The research and analysis branch was moved into the State Department's intelligence bureau and the remaining parts of the OSS were transferred to the war department and were renamed the Strategic Services unit. Because the OSS had been divided among these two groups, for a while each group fought over who would be in control of national intelligence. To resolve this, the president created the National Intelligence Authority, a panel of people from the army, navy, and State Department and from the Central Intelligence Group (CIG).

In July 1947 the National Security Act was put into effect and the Central Intelligence Agency was born. The agency answered to the president through the National Security Council, which was the organization that replaced the National Intelligence Authority. This organization was similar to the intelligence agency William Donovan recommended to President Roosevelt six years earlier. Some of the features from the earlier organizations were also part of the newly formed CIA.

The National Security Act defined the CIA's duties, which were mainly to make recommendations for coordinating intelligence, to evaluate intelligence from all areas, and to perform intelligence services that its other agencies were concerned about. The National Security Act also set certain requirements of the organization's director. It said that if the director who was chosen was a military officer, he would be freed from his military obligations and not allowed to serve in any military capacity while he was the director of the Central Intelligence Agency. The council also limited the CIA's work to encompass intelligence in only foreign countries and not in America. This helped the American people accept the CIA and reinforced the principle that the United States is a democracy.

Pierce Brosnan as James Bond. The day-to-day life of most operations officers gathering international intelligence is much less glamorous than Bond's.

CHAPTER **3**

How the Agency Works

THE CENTRAL INTELLIGENCE AGENCY'S main job is to collect information that helps keep our country safe. This job begins with a request from one of our country's leaders, such as the president, who asks the CIA to get some information. When the CIA is asked to do a job, it is **tasked.**

Each time the CIA is tasked, the situation is similar to starting a new puzzle at the dining room table. Just like the puzzles you find in the toy store, intelligence puzzles come in different shapes and sizes, which make up the different categories of intelligence. Current intelligence deals with events that are taking place in the world today. Estimative intelligence assesses what might happen in the future. Research intelligence is a detailed study of one issue or topic. Scientific and technical intelligence studies information on the technology of foreign countries. Warning intelligence notifies the nation's leaders that something might happen that will need their immediate attention.

All of these categories represent different types of puzzles. When the CIA is tasked, it first determines what type of puzzle it is and then figures out how to solve the puzzle. Intelligence is the sum of the answers the CIA gets. The CIA can be tasked for two reasons. These reasons are what the CIA calls its mission. Its mission is to provide accurate and timely intelligence on threats to America's security and to conduct counterintelligence to protect our nation's secrets when there is a threat to our national security.

The CIA has four divisions, or directorates. Each directorate has a team of people who work on one piece of the puzzle. When each team has completed its work, they join together to assemble the information. Like teams playing against each other in sports, there is some competitiveness between the directorates. Each directorate has its own mission, budget, and techniques. Sometimes, because of the competitiveness between directorates, some members of the groups feel that the work they do is more important than that done by the other directorates. This is not true. Although some directorates are more glamorous than others, without the information from every directorate, the intelligence puzzle would not be complete. The four directorates report to the director of the Central Intelligence Agency (DCI), who is the head of the CIA and in charge of the other agencies in the intelligence community. The DCI oversees the military intelligence agencies, the counterintelligence side of the FBI, and the National Security Council.

The Directorate of Operations is the best known branch of the CIA. The agents in this branch are the spies that most people think of when they learn about the agency. Although these people have been made famous in the movies and on television, it is hard for us to really know what the job of a person in this directorate is really like. Of all the divisions of the CIA, this one is the most secretive.

The people who work in this directorate are responsible for gathering intelligence through other people, rather than by reading newspapers or using satellites. People who work in this directorate usually live in a foreign country and are responsible for gathering information about that area. The world is divided into different regions, such as Western Europe and Latin America, and a chief who oversees each region and who reports back to CIA headquarters in the United States. Case officers, also called operations officers, are the men and women who have the job of the spies we most often see portrayed on film. These are the people who recruit agents who have access to the information that the CIA needs to help build their puzzle. Case officers usually work at other jobs as well to help maintain their cover.

When an operations officer recruits an agent, it is not up to just the officer to determine if the new agent is genuine. The counterintelligence staff under the directorate of operations also researches the person to determine if he or she is a good source. This group, based at CIA headquarters, has the job of being skeptical of every new agent and questioning whether he or she is a valid source of information. Sometimes an agent who claims to be helping the United States by providing information is actually helping another country by providing the Americans with false information. These agents are double agents. Differentiating between a person who is providing genuine information and one who is giving false information can be difficult. The counterintelligence staff's job also includes giving out false information to mislead foreign governments and to protect the United States. With several countries providing both accurate and false information at the same time, things can get very confusing, which is why this process is sometimes described as walking through a maze of mirrors.

In addition to operations, the Directorate of Science and Technology (DST) also collects information and supplies the tools to help the operations officers gather information. If you've seen a James Bond movie, just think of

"Q," the man who invents handy gadgets that always seem to rescue 007 from any dangerous situation. These tools include recording devices, tiny cameras, disguises, code-breaking equipment, and more. Some of the most interesting inventions are discussed in Chapter 5.

In addition to making the tools of the operations officers trade, the Directorate of Science and Technology also has other roles. A team with the Foreign Broadcast Information Service specializes in translating foreign newspapers and television and radio programs so that gov-

Translating foreign publications, such as these French newspapers describing the Cuban Missile Crisis of 1962, is part of the information-gathering work of the Directorate of Science and Technology.

ERECTORS REMOVED FROM LAUNCH POSITIONS

CAMOUFLAGED MISSILE TRANSPORTER REMOVED

LAUNCH STANDS REMAINING

CONTINUED CONSTRUCTION

ernment officials will have an accurate translation or a transcript of what was published or broadcast in a foreign country.

The National Photographic Interpretation Center looks at aerial photographs and decides what they mean. For example, in 1990 it was this center that first realized that Iraqi troops were moving toward Kuwait, three weeks before Kuwait was invaded. The photo interpreters saw that the Iraqi troops had taken along months' worth of fuel supplies, much more than would have been the case if they were doing just a training exercise. The center also provides information to other government agencies. Sometimes photo interpreters estimate the size of oil spills or forest fires; at other times they track the size of crops to make predictions on future harvests.

The Directorate of Science and Technology controls billion dollar satellites that can see through clouds and even through buildings. These satellites are very advanced compared to the ones that were first used. The first satellites

The 1962 Cuban Missile Crisis resulted when missile sites were discovered when analyzing aerial photographs of Cuba taken by United States reconnaissance planes.

ejected the film via parachute, requiring a plane to fly by and catch it in a bucket. Today, satellites transmit their pictures electronically. These satellites are powerful enough to read the numbers on a car license plate, but they are usually used to look at a much broader area. Because today's satellites transmit their images in real time, we can know the details of an incident, such as a terrorist attack, almost immediately after it has taken place.

The Directorate of Intelligence is the group that analyzes all the intelligence gathered by the Directorates of Operations and Science and Technology. These are the people who decide how the pieces of the puzzle fit together. Once the information is assembled, this directorate writes a variety of different reports that are sent to the National Intelligence Council. This group, in turn, gathers the reports of the Directorate of Intelligence and other groups within the intelligence community and creates reports that are given to the president.

Analyzing the information that has been gathered is not always easy. In the 1970s, the CIA needed to gather information about the Soviet economy, yet the Soviet government's statistics could not be trusted. Thus the CIA had to gather information and then make its own calculations.

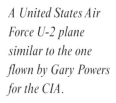

A United States Air Force U-2 plane similar to the one flown by Gary Powers for the CIA.

For example, when the CIA needed to estimate how much it cost to build a Soviet fighter plane, it added the cost of the steel to the cost of the labor to build the plane. The numbers were in Soviet money (called rubles), which the CIA then had to convert into dollars. Because there was no conversion rate between the dollars and rubles, the CIA had to make an estimate on what the conversion rate would be, based on what each currency could buy.

There were other challenges too. When people in the Directorate of Intelligence would write their reports, they would often use words like "likely," or "probably," but these words didn't give the director of Central Intelligence an accurate enough picture of what would happen. He wanted to know how likely something was to happen—for example, whether there was a 50 percent chance of an incident occurring.

When a piece of information is thoroughly analyzed and processed into a report, it is called **finished intelligence.** Finished intelligence includes only information considered to be important to government officials when

Gary Powers (second from right), the American U-2 pilot shot down while flying a CIA reconnaissance mission over the Soviet Union, on trial for espionage in 1962. Some CIA work involves high levels of risk.

they are making decisions. Two of the most important documents of finished intelligence are the National Intelligence Daily and the President's Daily Brief.

Produced by the National Foreign Assessment Center, the National Intelligence Daily is distributed every day to about 200 government officials. It explains the significance of the reports from secret sources within the current events of the world. The second document, the President's Daily Brief (PDB), is a short summary of the current intelligence and analysis that the president reads every morning in about 15 minutes. The purpose of this document is the same as that of the National Intelligence Daily. The difference is that the PDB goes to only a limited number of people and sometimes includes more secret information than what is contained in the National Intelligence Daily. Often, about half of the facts in the PDB have not as yet been publicized in newspapers or on television.

The Directorate of Administration, the fourth directorate, is the group that keeps the rest of the agency running. This is the team that ensures that the employees get paid, that computer equipment and phones are in the offices, and that the buildings have heat. Although they may not be the most glamorous of the directorates, they are very important. About 40 percent of the people who work for the CIA work in this directorate.

One of the most critical departments within the Directorate of Administration is the Office of Security. If you were to visit the CIA headquarters, a security officer would be the first person you would encounter. Dressed like park rangers, the guards greet everyone who comes to the CIA's gates, both employees and visitors. In addition to these duties, the Office of Security protects the director of the Central Intelligence Agency and regularly searches CIA offices all over the world for bugs and other spying devices.

Many of the departments within this directorate perform tasks that are typical in any company as well as ones that are unique to the CIA. For example, the Office of Medical Services gives physicals to employees, but they also perform psychological analyses of world leaders. The Office of Communications installs telephones in offices, but they also provide top-secret communications using satellites.

When all four directorates work together, they complete a process the CIA calls the intelligence cycle. This is the process in which raw information is turned into finished intelligence so officials from the United States government can use that intelligence to make decisions and take actions. The process begins with planning and direction. The CIA is asked to do a specific job at this stage.

The next step is collection. During this step the Directorate of Operations and the Directorate of Science and Technology gather the raw information. Although they gather some of this information secretly, most of it comes from **open sources,** such as newspapers, books, television broadcasts, and radio broadcasts. When the processing step takes place, the information is combined into a form that can be analyzed. Next, the Directorate of Intelligence converts the raw information into finished intelligence. Finally, it disseminates it to the government officials who initially requested the job.

The entrance to CIA
headquarters in McLean,
Virginia. Most of the CIA's
22,000 employees work here.

CHAPTER **4**

The People Behind the CIA

THE CENTRAL INTELLIGENCE AGENCY is not required to disclose how many employees it has, but experts estimate that about 22,000 people work for the agency. CIA employees are stationed in nearly every country in the world; the majority, however, work in or near Washington, D.C., including at the CIA headquarters in McLean, Virginia. Most of the employees are classified as "white." This means that these employees are overt, or that they can acknowledge that they work for the CIA but often cannot tell anyone what type of work they do.

The other group of employees, called "black," are employees who work on the **covert** side in the Directorate of Operations. Not only are they not allowed to say they work for the CIA, many of these employees have fake identities. Their names, family history, education, and other information are completely made up. If you were to send a letter to CIA headquarters, addressed to an officer working undercover, it would get returned, saying that there was no such person at the agency.

There are many different jobs within the agency, including those held by scientists, engineers, historians, economists, lawyers, physicians, and chemists. The only requirement to work for the CIA is to be a United States citizen. Getting a job at the agency, however, is very difficult. Only about 1 percent of the people who apply are actually offered jobs. Every applicant must pass a lie detector test and a physical examination before he or she is hired. All employees must also agree to a code of silence, which says that they cannot discuss their jobs—or any other aspect of the CIA—with anyone else in any detail. They also must sign an agreement that says that anything they write about their work must be submitted to CIA censors. The agency is so secretive that things that would not normally be considered privileged information are that at the agency. Even items such as newspaper articles are sometimes stamped "secret."

The person who oversees all of the employees is the director of central intelligence (DCI). This person is the leader of the CIA as well as of the entire intelligence community and is an important figure in the United States government. Before the DCI goes into his office for the day, he sometimes visits the White House. An armored car picks him up at his home. At around 8:00 A.M. he meets with the president to give him the President's Daily Brief (PDB). Depending on the president's preference, the DCI may deliver the PDB directly to the president or he may present it to one of the president's national security advisers. Sometimes instead of the DCI, a briefer, a person who works in the department that prepares the PDB, may deliver the President's Daily Brief. During the Gulf War, the director of central intelligence, William Webster,

met with President George Bush everyday to deliver the PDB.

The PDB is usually an eight- to ten-page document with newspaper-style columns. It is bound together like a book. The left-hand pages usually contain photographs or charts; the right-hand pages contain text. It is prepared by a group of people who send it to the CIA's own printing plant at 5:30 A.M. each morning. Once it is printed, it is sealed, and two copies are delivered; one to the DCI's house and a second to the White House. The PDB began with President John F. Kennedy, who asked for a document that discussed his precise interests and that was shorter than the National Intelligence Daily, another similar document. It is up to each president to determine who will receive the PDB every day. President Bush, for example, had copies

During the Gulf War, the director of central intelligence met with President George Bush daily to provide him with information needed for Pentagon briefings such as this one in 1990.

distributed to his secretaries of defense and state and to the chairman of the Joint Chiefs of Staff.

Just as the president decides who gets the PDB, he also decides who he wants in the position of director of central intelligence. The Senate must approve this appointment. The president also appoints the deputy director of central intelligence and, like the DCI, this person oversees both the CIA and the entire intelligence community. Reporting to the DCI are four deputy directors (one for each of the directorates) and several staff offices that work directly for him. They include people who write speeches, handle media requests, and monitor compliance of arms control agreements.

Everyday thousands of CIA employees report to headquarters near Washington, D.C. Located on 225 acres, the concrete and glass complex is made up of two buildings with a total of two-and-a-half million square feet. The main entrance has 15 doors, which lead to a lobby constructed of gray and white marble. Signs from the nearby highways direct visitors to the CIA compound, which is surrounded by a double chain-link fence that is topped by barbed wire. Security at the complex is tight. Guard dogs and security people who carry machine guns protect the site. The fence that surrounds the complex has a special security system that sounds an alarm when the fence vibrates.

Headquarters is often referred to as "Langley," after the town Langley, Virginia, which no longer exists. In the early 1900s, Langley was a small village with a country store, an inn, and a post office. By 1910, however, the village was merged with McLean, a neighboring town, and the Langley post office was closed. Today the CIA has its own zip code. Mail is routed into the Washington, D.C., post office, where it can be screened by X-ray equipment before it is delivered to the compound. When mail arrives

at the agency's loading dock, a second X-ray machine checks the packages.

The people who work for the Office of Security are in charge of the building's safety. These jobs, however, are only slightly similar to the jobs held by typical security officers. About 100 technicians in this department spend most of their time looking for bugs and other eavesdropping devices in CIA buildings around the world. Two technicians may take one or more weeks to **sweep** a CIA station looking for bugs. Because there are so many places that eavesdropping devices can be hidden, technicians must practice their skills. To do this, CIA employees from the Office of Technical Service hide bugs, and the debugging technicians practice finding them.

The smallest group of employees works in the Directorate of Intelligence. Most of the people who work in this division are analysts. Their jobs are similar to those of

CIA employees entering the headquarters building must pass through a security area staffed by Office of Security members.

college professors. These people often specialize and become experts in one area. Sometimes they even write articles in academic magazines and speak at conferences. The analysts have been criticized occasionally over the years. At times they have been criticized for being too specific and for overemphasizing relatively unimportant events. At other times they have been criticized for not being specific enough and for offering only general predictions about certain events.

Not all of the employees at the CIA are human. In the center courtyard at the CIA compound, a robot is used to cut the grass. The Office of Security uses guard dogs to help protect the agency from intruders. Dogs are also used to sniff out explosives and other items that might be dangerous. These dogs are part of the CIA's Canine Corps, which is similar to the K-9 unit at a local police station. Each dog has a handler who trains with the dog. The dog and its handler are partners and are called in on special missions, such as after the bombing that occurred during the 1996 Summer Olympics in Atlanta, Georgia.

The Canine Corps dogs train at CIA headquarters as well as at other places, such as sports arenas. Every dog and his handler go through 13 weeks of training to learn how to search for different types of explosives. Some then train for another 13 weeks to learn how to search people and places as well as how to apprehend a suspect. Being a member of the Canine Corps is hard work. The dogs are on call all the time and work 60 hours a week, but they are very well cared for. Every dog lives with his or her handler and the handler's family, even after the dog retires from service.

The most elite job at the CIA is that of operations officer. These men and women are stationed all over the world. Not only is their work sometimes dangerous, they are often away from their families, which can be very difficult for the officer as well as for their families. Most opera-

A dog trained to sniff out fire-starting liquids assists in an arson investigation.

tions officers are men, because in foreign countries women are often not accepted in certain positions. Operations officers almost always have some type of cover so no one will know they work for the CIA. The cover may be as simple as saying they work for the U.S. embassy or it may involve a new identity with a fake company.

The officer is often allowed to bring his family with him when he is sent on an assignment, which typically lasts two years. The family may live in the country where the officer is assigned. If it is too dangerous there, however, the family may live in a nearby country, with the officer returning home as often as he can to visit. Such a situation puts a strain on many families and often results in divorce.

Parachuting is part of the special training a new CIA officer must undergo during his or her first year of service.

The CIA recruits its operations officers in the same way that it recruits its other employees. CIA recruiters place ads in major newspapers and go to college campuses and job fairs. Applicants are thinned out first through phone interviews, next via resumés, and then through a series of in-person interviews. Applicants who make it that far must undergo three days of extensive tests, including a medical exam and a polygraph test. If the person is still a possible candidate, then the CIA does an extensive background check on the person. Taking several months, background checks can become as detailed as questioning the applicant's elementary school teachers.

Once an officer accepts a job, he trains for two years before he goes on his first tour, an overseas assignment. When the person is first hired, he joins a group of new officers for one year of special training in surveillance, parachuting, electronics, a foreign language, and so on. During the second year the new officer works at headquarters as a support person for one of the stations overseas.

Although being an operations officer is the most elite position a person can hold at the CIA, the CIA recruits only the best, brightest, and most outstanding candidates for every position. If you work for the CIA, no matter what your job is, you can take pride in knowing that you work at one of the most exclusive government agencies in the United States.

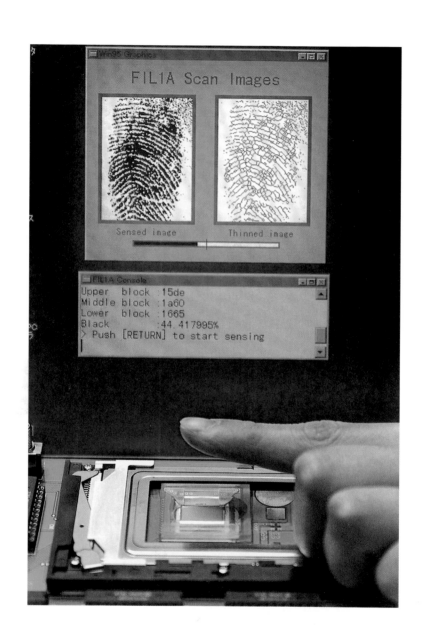

The first microchip capable of identifying fingerprints electronically, developed by a Japanese communications company. A fingerprint can be "sensed" in half a second with 99 percent accuracy.

CHAPTER **5**

Gadgets and Gizmos

JUST AS "Q" DOES in the James Bond films, the Directorate of Science and Technology (DST) has hundreds of employees who build devices to help the operations officers do their job of spying better. They make devices that help the officers eavesdrop on conversations, take pictures without anyone knowing they're doing so, pick locks, and even protect themselves with small weapons. To prevent their devices from being discovered, the DST also creates ways to conceal their items in toolboxes, paintings, toiletry kits—even in teddy bears. Fascinating gadgets and gizmos are designed to do all sorts of things that help officers perform their job of spying without getting caught.

Much of the communication an officer has with his agents and with other officers must be secret. Meeting in person with anyone to get or give information is very dangerous, so different devices have been created to allow communication without face-to-face meetings. Officers may need to get verbal information from someone else, but they need to make sure that no one else hears that information. Special radios may be used for this type of communication. Created in the 1920s, these radios were used often during World War II and were sometimes built into suitcases or briefcases so they could be carried in the open. Using these radios, officers often sent messages in Morse code. Depending on the type of antenna that was used, messages could be transmitted a distance of between 300 and 3,000 miles. When officers sent messages over a long distance, in addition to using Morse code they sometimes used burst encoding. In burst encoding the message is sent in short bursts, making it less likely to be detected.

Spying equipment from the 1960s: a listening device planted in a talcum powder container and a communications radio built into a briefcase.

When messages were sent in written form, other methods were used to make sure no one interpreted the message. Sometimes messages were written in code or using secret writing. Secret writing might be done by using a chemical or an invisible ink and writing on a piece of cloth or in between the lines of a normal letter. The person who receives the message then uses a chemical or heat to expose the secret writing. To protect the message even further, the sender may write it in code using a cipher, a technique in which letters are substituted using a special system so only the person who knows the code can interpret the message.

An American inventor named Edward Hebern began making cipher machines in 1909 as a way for businesspeople who were worried about competing companies stealing their secrets to communicate. In 1915 he made a cipher using two typewriters that were connected electronically to a rotating disk in the center. The message would be typed on one typewriter normally and it would automatically be printed in code on the second typewriter. Although this machine was very advanced, the United States Navy was able to break the code. He kept working on his invention and eventually created the most secure cipher machine used in World War II.

In addition to communicating in secret, operations officers also need to listen to conversations and watch people's movements. Sometimes the listening devices are hidden in a person's clothing. At other times they are hidden in walls, lamps, pens, books, and so on. When these devices were first used, they had to be strong enough to transmit the audio information to the person who was listening nearby, but they had to be weak enough so they couldn't be detected by someone who was searching for bugs. Today, listening devices can store the audio files using digital technology and then transmit the files to someone at a scheduled time.

Similarly, special tools have been made to allow people to watch others without their knowledge. In the early 1800s the French made a set of binoculars that had an angled mirror on one side. When a person looked through them, he seemed to be looking straight ahead. In fact, however, the person was really watching someone off to his right. Today there are night vision devices that work with existing light and allow the viewer to see when it is almost completely dark.

An officer can also use various items to enter a locked building without anyone's knowledge. There are lock-pick tools and electronic lock-pick kits to unlock doors and other objects. There are also devices to copy a key quickly and return it before anyone becomes suspicious. Once the spy is inside the building, he or she sometimes needs to gather information from documents. To avoid detection, the documents are often photographed or copied and interpreted later. Spies have used tiny cameras hidden in watches, purses, umbrellas, and even cigarette lighters, for many years. Other cameras can be rolled over a sheet of paper or a book to literally copy the contents.

One of the most famous types of cameras is the Minox subminiature camera, invented by Walter Zapp, a Latvian. The first Minox camera was made in 1938. It could take 50 pictures in a roll of film one-quarter the size of a 35mm roll. To take pictures of documents, spies often used a copy stand or a measuring chain to make sure that the distance was the same every time, so all the pictures would be in focus.

Because intelligence agencies all over the world have numerous devices for spying, every agency has a team of experts that specializes in counterintelligence methods to make sure that their secrets are safe. A member of this team can use equipment to search for bugs, uncover radio-

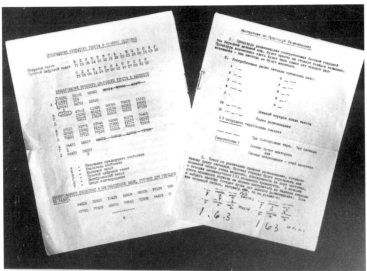

Spy equipment used by a Soviet double agent. The top half of the photograph shows pages from a code book. Minox subminiature cameras are shown at bottom, in front of the transistor radio set.

transmitting signals, or determine if someone has been in the room or not.

Chemicals can be dusted onto objects, such as door-knobs or documents, to help determine who has touched them. The chemicals become invisible on the objects, but still get transferred to the hands of anyone who touches them. When an ultraviolet light is held up to the skin, the chemical becomes visible.

To check a room for bugs, technicians use anti bug-ging devices consisting of a radio receiver linked with other electronics equipment. Because these devices only

DNA testing can be used to identify fingerprints found at crime scenes.

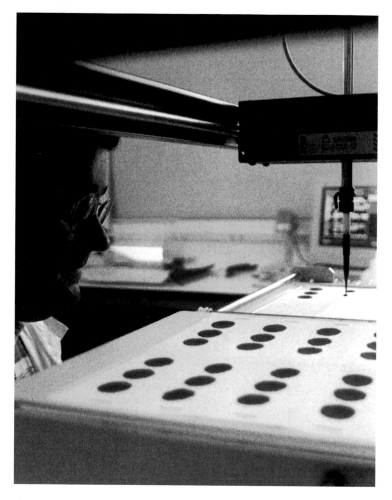

detect bugs that are in the process of transmitting, the area must also be checked for bugs that are not currently transmitting.

Sometimes counterintelligence officers must intercept communications that are being sent by the enemy. To do this, officers may search through the mail, looking for letters to or from suspected enemy spies. In some countries, including the United States, officers need a special warrant to do this. When they intercept these letters, they want to know the contents without alerting the sender or the recipient to the fact that the letter has been intercepted. During World War II, spies inserted a special tool into the tiny gap at the top of the envelope flap. They rolled the letter around the tool and removed it through the opening. Because very thin writing paper was used at that time, this was a lot easier to do then than it would be today.

Benjamin Franklin was a member of the first foreign intelligence team of the United States, which had its own courier system and secret navy.

Famous People

MANY PEOPLE HAVE BEEN involved with American espionage since the time our country was founded. Some people had official jobs, others simply helped gather information because they felt it would help the country. One of the earliest spies in American history was Benjamin Franklin. In addition to helping draft the Declaration of Independence, Franklin served on several secret committees within the Continental Congress.

One of these committees was the Committee of Secret Correspondence, which is considered by some to be the first foreign intelligence team of the United States. Franklin and the other members of the committee recruited agents overseas and created a courier system to get information. They even organized a secret navy to deliver military supplies. A short time later Franklin joined the Committee of Secret Correspondence. This committee obtained and distributed military supplies.

When Franklin went overseas, much of his work there was conducting espionage activities. In France, while officially negotiating an alliance with the French, he was also gathering intelligence, recruiting new agents, and distributing propaganda.

Another important man in early American intelligence was James Armistead Lafayette, who was a slave in Virginia when America was fighting for independence from the British. He got permission to join General Lafayette, whom he idolized. He pretended to be an escaped slave and was recruited by the British to spy on the Americans. He became a double agent, staying loyal to America. After the Revolutionary War, James was freed from slavery because of all of his work as a spy .

Another unlikely spy was Morris (Moe) Berg, a baseball player for the Brooklyn Dodgers and a few other teams. In 1934, using his real job playing baseball as a cover, Berg went to Tokyo, Japan, and took still and motion pictures of production plants that were making weapons and ammunition. These pictures were critical eight years later, when Lieutenant Colonel James Doolittle was planning the first American air strike against Japan after the attack on Pearl Harbor.

In 1942, at the request of President Franklin D. Roosevelt, General William Donovan formed the Office of Strategic Services (OSS). Moe Berg became one of William Donovan's first recruits for this organization, which was the first formal intelligence service in the United States. Moe worked on some of the most dangerous missions of the time, traveling overseas frequently. On one mission he convinced Italian and German scientists to come to America and help develop its space and atomic programs. Berg is believed to have continued working on dangerous espionage missions well into his sixties.

Although it was unusual for a woman to be involved in espionage at the time, Helene Deschamps, a French woman who worked for several years in the French Resistance, came to work for the OSS in 1943. Helene and her adopted sister Jackie Bouquier had no formal training as spies, but they were accepted by the OSS almost immediately. During World War II, background checks or other approval methods were nonexistent. Helene spent years as a spy on many dangerous missions. She worked to find the locations of minefields, gathered information on enemy troops, and learned details of troop movements during the war.

After World War II, William Donovan urged President Roosevelt to create an intelligence organization similar to the OSS but that would be a permanent part of the government, to assist in both times of peace and of war. Although Roosevelt listened to Donovan's advice, the project was never started. In 1945, when President Harry S. Truman was in office, he disbanded the OSS, which left Donovan without a job. In 1947, using many of Donovan's ideas, President Truman officially formed the CIA as we know it today.

President Truman appointed Rear Admiral Sidney Souers the first director of central intelligence in January 1946. At the time, the organization was called the Central Intelligence Group and fell under the guidance of the National Intelligence Authority. Souers agreed to stay in the position for six months, which he and the president felt was long enough to get the group organized. As agreed upon, he left the position in June 1946.

One of the first female operations officers was Virginia Hall, who had served as an intelligence agent for the OSS. An expert in Morse code and radio operations, she was awarded the Distinguished Service Cross, the second highest United States military honor. Hall was the only female civilian in the war to receive this medal of honor. She went on to work for the CIA for many years, leaving only because she reached the mandatory retirement age.

Former President George Bush (center), flanked by CIA Director George Tenet (left) and Barbara Bush (right), at a 1999 ceremony renaming CIA headquarters the George Bush Center for Intelligence.

Called "America's first professional spy," Allen Dulles worked for the OSS and was part of the committee that had advised President Truman when he created the Central Intelligence Agency. In 1952 he was appointed to the top position at the CIA. Dulles was one of the best spies America had, but when he was put in charge of the CIA, he did not do well. He was forced to resign as director after his plan for the Bay of Pigs invasion in Cuba failed.

Over the next decade the CIA had many challenging times. The agency was not highly thought of by the public, by other government agencies, and even by its employees. In January 1976 President Gerald Ford chose George Bush as the interim director of the CIA. It was Bush's job to bolster morale and to continue the work that the prior DCI, William Colby, had begun. Bush's role as director was short-lived, however. After President Carter took office, he appointed Stansfield Turner to the position. Bush left the position in March 1977 and later became vice president and then president of the United States. In 1999 the CIA headquarters in McLean, Virginia, was renamed the George Bush Center for Intelligence.

Over the years, many Americans have given their lives for their country as a result of being caught spying. In modern times, the people who have died as a result of their espionage activities are immortalized on the wall of stars in the lobby of the CIA's headquarters. Each individual is thought of as a true American hero, in the spirit of Nathan Hale, the first American captured and killed for spying. Just before he died, he said to the British executioner, "I only regret I have but one life to lose for my country."

Chronology

1941   President Franklin D. Roosevelt appoints William J. Donovan the coordinator of information.

1942   Roosevelt establishes the Offices of Strategic Services (OSS) and names William J. Donovan its director.

1946   President Harry S. Truman establishes the Central Intelligence Group to operate under the National Intelligence Authority with Rear Admiral Sidney W. Souers as its director.

1947   The National Security Act of 1947 establishes the National Security Council, and the Central Intelligence Agency replaces the National Intelligence Authority and the Central Intelligence Group.

1955   President Dwight D. Eisenhower signs a bill authorizing $46 million for the construction of a CIA headquarters building.

1975   The Senate forms what became known as the Church Committee, headed by Senator Frank Church. This committee investigates intelligence activities for 15 months and submits its final report to the public in April 1976.

1978   The intelligence community is reorganized by President Carter, who places the director of central intelligence in charge of the operations and budget of the entire intelligence community.

1982   President Ronald Reagan signs the Intelligence Identities Protection Act, which allows criminal charges to be brought against anyone who reveals the names of covert intelligence employees.

1984   The Central Intelligence Agency Information Act is signed by President Reagan, making the CIA exempt from releasing classified files, which would normally be required by the Freedom of Information Act.

1999   The CIA headquarters in McLean, Virginia, is renamed the George Bush Center for Intelligence.

Glossary

Case officer—An agent in charge of operations at a CIA station; also called an operations officer.

Cipher—A technique in which letters are substituted using a system so that only someone who knows the code can interpret the message.

Clandestine—Secret.

Counterintelligence—Operations to protect the United States information, equipment, and overseas operations from sabotage or foreign intelligence.

Covert—A secret or undercover activity.

Double agent—A person who is working for two opposing organizations at once, being loyal to one and betraying the secrets of the other.

Finished intelligence—Intelligence that has been analyzed and presented in a report to government officials.

Open sources—Sources of information that are available to the public, such as newspapers, radio broadcasts, and television broadcasts.

Overt—Another word for open as in sources or people who can acknowledge they work for the CIA.

Scout—Another term for spy; used during the Civil War.

Sweep—The process followed by technicians to check a room for eavesdropping devices.

Tasked—The term CIA employees use when they have been given an assignment by a government official.

Further Reading

Aaseng, Nathan. *Treacherous Traitors.* Minneapolis, MN: The Oliver Press, 1997.

Deschamps, Helene, and Monget, Karyn, Editor. *Spyglass.* New York: Henry Holt, 1995.

Dulles, Allen. *The Craft of Intelligence.* New York: Harper & Row, 1963.

Gaines, Ann G. *Terrorism.* Philadelphia: Chelsea House, 1999.

Jeffreys-Jones, Rhodri. *The CIA and American Democracy.* New Haven, CT: Yale University Press, 1989.

Kessler, Ronald. *Inside the CIA.* New York: Pocket Books, 1994.

Melton, H. Keith. *The Ultimate Spy Book.* New York: DK Publishing, 1996.

Meyer, Cord. *Facing Reality: From World Federalism to the CIA.* New York: Harper & Row, 1980.

Nash, Jay Robert. *Spies: A Narrative Encyclopedia of Dirty Deeds and Double Dealing from Biblical Times to Today.* New York: Evans, 1997.

O'Toole, G. J. A. *The Encyclopedia of American Intelligence and Espionage, from the Revolutionary War to the Present.* New York: Facts on File, 1988.

Payne, Ronald, and Dobson, Christopher. *Who's Who In Espionage.* New York: St. Martin's Press, 1984.

Ranelagh, John. *The Agency: The Rise and Decline of the CIA.* New York: Simon and Schuster, 1986.

Volkman, Ernest. *Espionage: The Greatest Spy Operation of the Twentieth Century.* New York: Wiley, 1995.

Wise, David. *Molehunt: The Secret Search for Traitors That Shattered the CIA.* New York: Random House, 1992.

Ziff, John. *Espionage and Treason.* Philadelphia: Chelsea House, 2000.

Index

ABOUT THE AUTHOR: Tara Baukus Mello is a freelance writer who has published over 1500 articles. She has also written seven books, including this one: *George Washington, John Smith, Mark Martin, Rusty Wallace, Stunt Driving,* and *The Pit Crew*—all published by Chelsea House. A graduate of Harvard University, she lives in southern California with her husband Jeff and her dog Tyler.

ACKNOWLEDGMENTS: The author would like to thank Christina Baukus for her research assistance with this book as well as Chase Brandon for sharing his extensive knowledge and passion for the CIA and espionage with children throughout the country.

SENIOR CONSULTING EDITOR Arthur M. Schlesinger, jr. is the leading American historian of our time. He won the Pulitzer Prize for his book *The Age of Jackson* (1945) and again for *A Thousand Days* (1965). This chronicle of the Kennedy Administration also won a National Book Award. Professor Schlesinger is the Albert Schweitzer Professor of the Humanities at the City University of New York, and has been involved in several other Chelsea House projects, including the REVOLUTIONARY WAR LEADERS and COLONIAL LEADERS series.

Picture Credits

page
8: Reuters/Jeff Mitchell/ Archive Photos
11: Archive Photos
13: Archive Photos
14: Roger Ressmeyer/Corbis
16: Archive Photos
19: Archive Photos
20: Archive Photos
21: Archive Photos
23: Scott Swanson/ Archive Photos

26: Archive Photos
30: Agence France Presse/ Archive Photos
31: Archive Photos
32: Archive Photos
33: Archive Photos
36: Roger Ressmeyer/Corbis
39: Reuters/Gary Cameron/ Archive Photos
41: Roger Ressmeyer/Corbis
43: AP/Wide World Photos

44: Crady von Pawlak/ Archive Photos
46: AP/Wide World Photos
48: Agence France Presse/ Archive Photos
51: AP/Wide World Photos
52: AP/Wide World Photos
54: Lambert/Archive Photos
58: Reuters/Kevin Lamarque/Archive Photos